Good News of Great Joy

A MUSICAL CHRISTMAS CELEBRATION

Created and Arranged by
Bill and Robin Wolaver

Narration by Robin Wolaver

FOREWORD

Last December, we watched in joy and amazement as country after country opened their hearts to the celebration of Christmas. People who for generations had either celebrated secretly or not at all, were suddenly given freedom to openly proclaim the good news of Christ's birth.

It was seeing the hand of God move in such a dramatic fashion that spurred us to write this musical. Never before in history has there been greater opportunity to evangelize, and we must take advantage of it. The people of the world are in desperate need of the gospel of Jesus, and it is our prayer that this work will serve as a tool, helping music ministries everywhere take the "Good News of Great Joy" to all people.

Bill and Robin Wolaver

CONTENTS

Christmas Calls for a Celebration

with **"O Come, Let Us Adore Him"**

Robin Wolaver, Julie Adams, and Nancy Gordon

Bill Wolaver
Arr. by Bill Wolaver

15
1st time: Choir unison (soprano part)
2nd time: Parts
one, come all, come join the glad oc - ca - sion.
thanks, re - joice, dark - ness has now been bro - ken. The
2. Give thanks, re - joice,
15
F
C/F
B♭/F
C/F F C/D Dm7
19
Come hon - or Him with joy - ful hearts; give praise and ad - o -
Child of love, this spe - cial One ful - fills the prom - ise
19
B♭
F/A
Gm7
D/F♯ Dsus/E D
Gm Gm/B♭ D/A Gm
Parts: both times
24
ra - tion.
spo - ken.
Rise up and sing;
O come, a - dore
Rise up and sing;
O come, a - dore
all
the
B♭/C
C
B♭/C
C
24
F
C/F

28
peo - ple of ev - 'ry na - tion are of - fered His in - vi - ta - tion. Christ - mas
Mak - er of all cre - a - tion, born to be our sal - va - tion. Christ - mas
B♭/F C/F F Am7 F/A
28
B♭add9 C C/D Dm
32
div. f
calls!
calls!
Christ - mas calls for a cel - e -
div. f
unis.
Gm11 F/A B♭ B♭/C C
32
B♭/F F F/A
f
36
bra - tion!
Christ - mas calls for a cel - e -
div.
F/B♭ B♭ F B♭ F B♭ F
36
Gm11/9 Gm Gm/F C7/E C7

40
mf
bra - tion!
Hope to all peo-ple He brings,
Bb/F F D/F# Gm D/F#
40
mf
44
Je-sus, our heav-en-ly King. Let the bells of glad - ness ring.
mf
Dm/F C/E A/C# A7/C# Dm C/E F D/F#
44
f
CD:3
CD:4 (2nd time)
unis.
1
Ladies mf
Christ - mas calls for a cel - e - bra - tion! 2. Give
unis.
Gm F/A Bb Bbadd9/C F9sus F Bb/F C/F
f

2
52
mp Warmly
bra - tion!
Cel - e -
F
F
E♭
D♭M7
mp
brate the ho - ly birth, the
E♭
D♭M7
E♭
56
div.
mir - a - cle of His life.
D♭M7
D♭
E♭
E♭
A♭

60
mf
Cel - e - brate the
C/G
Dm/G
poco a poco cresc.
64
light that shone that won - der - ful Christ - mas
C/G
Dm/G
G/F
C/E
Dm7
G
CD:5
mp unis.
night!
O
O
mf unis.
B♭/C
C
B♭/C
C
B♭/C
B♭
C/B♭
F/A
Gm7
smoothly

70
* "O Come, Let Us Adore Him" (Traditional - John Francis Wade)
come, a - dore!
come, let us a - dore
F
C/F
F
F9sus
mp
grad. cresc.
74
Come one, come all!
Him. O come, let us a -
C(no3)/F
Bb/F
mf
div.
78
O come, let
dore Him.
Gm

us a - dore Him.
C/E
G7/D
C
C/B♭
F/A
B♭
84
CD:6
unis.
Christ - mas calls for a cel - e -
unis.
B♭ F B♭ F B♭ F B♭ F/A
Gm F/A B♭
B♭add9/C
bra - tion!
88
f
div.
Christ - mas calls for a cel - e -
Dsus
D
C/G G
G/B
f

92
bra - tion!
Christ - mas calls for a cel - e -
div.
G/C C G C G C G Am9(11) Am Am/G D7/F♯ D7
92
96
bra - tion!
Hope to all peo - ple He brings,
C/G G E/G♯ Am E/G♯
96
Je - sus, our heav - en - ly King. Let the bells of glad - ness ring.
Em/G D/F♯ B/D♯ B7/D♯ Em D/F♯ G G/F E E/D

102
Christ - mas calls,
Christ - mas calls,
102
Am/C E/B Am C/D D/C Bm Bm7 D/E E7
106
Christ - mas calls
unis. ff
for a cel - e -
unis.
106
Am7 G/B C C/D
ff
110
bra - tion!
div. ff
Cel - e - bra - tion!
div.
110
C/G G E♭/B♭ B♭ F/C C C/D G
ff

Narr. 1: The Lord is worthy of praise, *(music begins)* for He has come and has redeemed His people. (Luke 1:68)

Narr. 2: Give praise to the Lord, who has loved us with an everlasting love. He has given heaven's greatest treasure, His precious Son, that we might have hope for eternity and peace in a troubled world. (Jeremiah 31:3 & John 3:16)

Narr. 1: The good news of the Christmas story is rich in truth and power. With the dawn of each new generation, the joyful message of the Messiah's birth reaches deep into searching hearts.

Narr. 2: It speaks of hope to the hopeless.

Narr. 1: It offers strength to the wounded.

Narr. 2: It whispers rest to the weary.

Narr. 1: It sings of love to the unloved.

Narr. 2: Christmas comes with open arms and eagerly invites us back through the pages of history, to witness the awesome wonder of God's unfailing love . . . to witness the miracle of . . .

Narr. 1 & 2: Emmanuel, God with us!

The First Noel

(Narration underscore)

Traditional

Arr. by Bill Wolaver

O Come, Little Children

Christoph von Schmidt

Johann A. P. Schulz
Arr. by Bill Wolaver

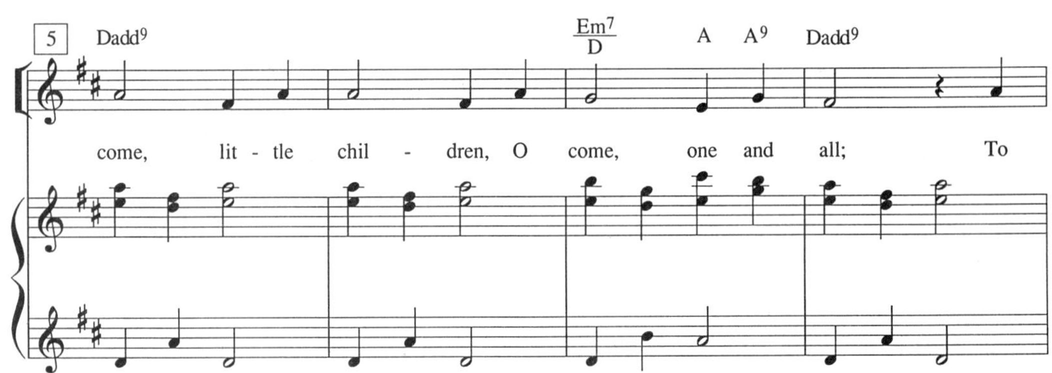

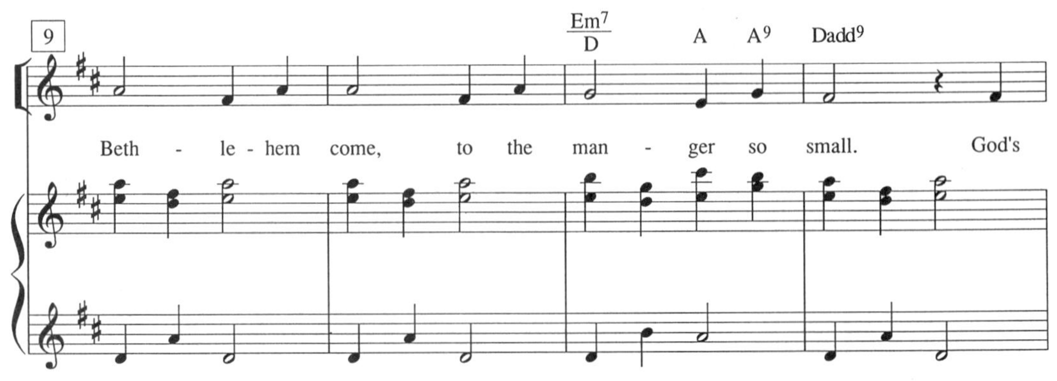

13
A
A/C♯
Em
Em/G
Bm
Bm/D
Son for a gift has been sent you this
G
17
D/A
A/G
night To be your Re -
D/F♯
G
A7
20
Dadd9
DM7
deem - er, your joy and de - light.
F♯m7
DM7/F♯
GM7
A7
Segue to
"Tell Me the Story of Jesus"

Tell Me the Story of Jesus

Fanny J. Crosby
2nd vs. by Julie Adams

John R. Sweney
Arr. by Bill Wolaver

Narr. 1: Christmas offers a special opportunity to share the good news of the Savior's birth.

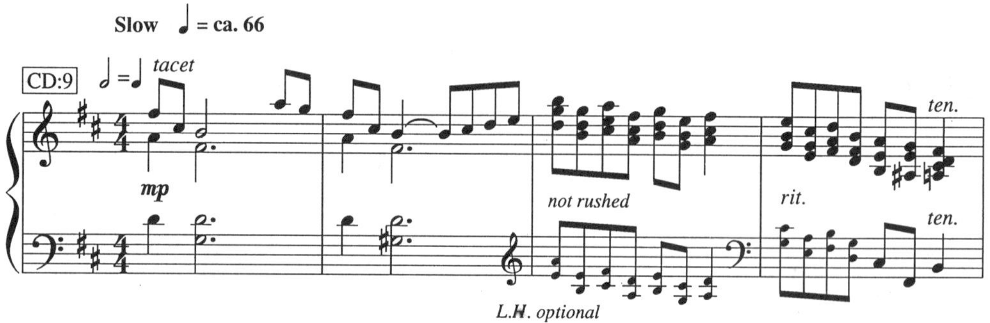

Narr. 2: This holiday season, may Christ be the center of our celebration. As we relax at home with family or enjoy time spent with friends, may the wonderful story of Jesus be on our lips and in our thoughts.

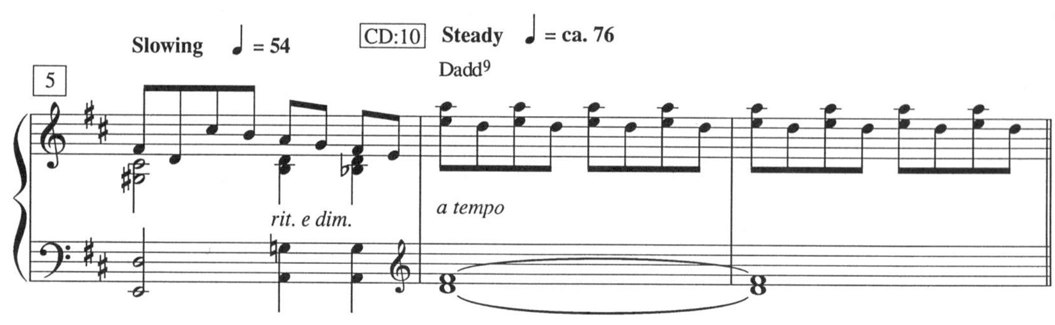

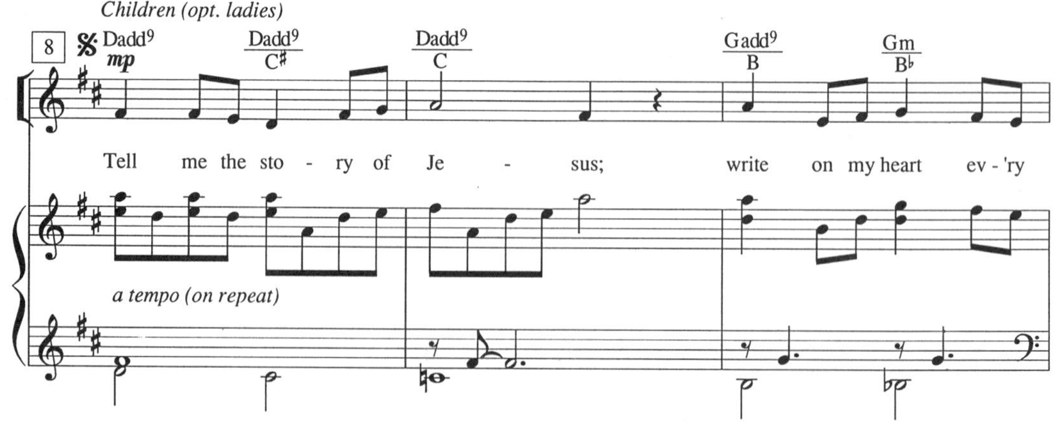

Dadd9
G/A
12
D
Em7
F♯m7
A/B
B7
Em7
G/A
A13/9♭
word. Tell me the sto - ry most pre - cious, sweet - est that ev - er was
heard.
2nd time to Coda
16
Ladies div.
mf
Tell how the an - gels in cho - rus
D7
2nd time to Coda
16
G
G/D
D
mf
sang as they wel - comed His birth,
20
"Glo - ry to God in the
Men div. mf
Gadd9/A
A7
A/C♯
D
D7
20
G

CD:11
unis.
slight rit.
D.S. al Coda
high - est! Peace and good tid - ings to earth."
unis.
G/D D A/E DM7/E D/E E9 Gadd9/A A13 9♭
D.S. al Coda
slight rit.
Coda Choir (parts)
mf
Tell how the Lord of sal - va - tion
Coda G G/D D
mf
came in the form of a Babe;
Gadd9/A A7 A/C♯ D D7

28
CD:12
unis.
Tell how the star in the heav - ens bright - ened the sta - ble where He
unis.
28
G
G/D
D
A/E
DM7/E
D/E
E9
Add children (opt.)
32
mf
div.
lay.
Tell me the sto - ry of Je - sus;
div.
Gadd9/A
A♭add9/B♭
B♭7
32
E♭add9
E♭/D
E♭/D♭
mf
36
(opt. cues for children)
write on my heart ev - 'ry word.
Tell me the sto - ry most
A♭add9/C
A♭m/C♭
E♭add9/B♭
A♭/B♭
36
E♭
Fm7

* If desired, children may exit here.

Mary's Little Boy Chile

J.H.

Jester Hairston
Arr. by Bill Wolaver

Beth - le-hem, so the Ho - ly Bi - ble say,
Am/G
D/G
G
13
Ma - ry's boy chile, Je - sus Christ, was born on Christ - mas day.
13
G/B
C
Am7
G/D
D7
G
17
While shep - herds watched their flocks by night, they saw a
Men unison mp
17
Am/G

21
bright new shin - ing star
And heard a choir from
D/G
G
21
G/B
heav - en sing;
the mu - sic came from a - far.
C
Am7
G/D
D7
G
25
Choir (parts)
mf
Hark! Now hear the an - gels sing,
"New King is born to - day,
25
G
C
D
B
Em
A
D
mf

29
unis.
And man will live for - ev - er-more be -
unis.
29
G
G/B
C
Am7
CD:14
cause of Christ - mas day."
Now
G/D
D7
G
E♭
D♭add9/E♭
34
Jo - seph and his wife, Ma - ry, came to Beth - le - hem that night.
34
A♭
B♭m/A♭
E♭/A♭

38
They found no place to bear her chile; not a
A♭
38
A♭/C
D♭
B♭m7
sin - gle room was in sight.
42
By and by they found a
A♭/E♭
E♭7
A♭
42
lit - tle nook in a sta - ble all for-lorn,
And
B♭m/A♭
E♭/A♭
A♭

46
in a man - ger cold and dark, Ma-ry's lit - tle boy chile was born.
46
A♭/C
D♭
B♭m7
A♭/E♭
E♭7
A♭
50
div.
f
Hark! Now hear the an - gels sing,
div.
50
A♭
D♭
E♭
C
f
unis.
54
"New King is born to - day, And man will live for -
unis.
Fm
B♭
E♭
54
A♭
A♭/C

CD:15
ev - er-more be - cause of Christ - mas day."
D♭ B♭m7 A♭/E♭ E♭7 A♭ E7
58
div. f
Trum - pets sound and an - gels sing; lis-ten to what they say,
div.
58
A D E C♯ F♯m B E
f
unis.
62
That man will live for - ev - er-more be -
unis.
62 A A/C♯ D Bm7

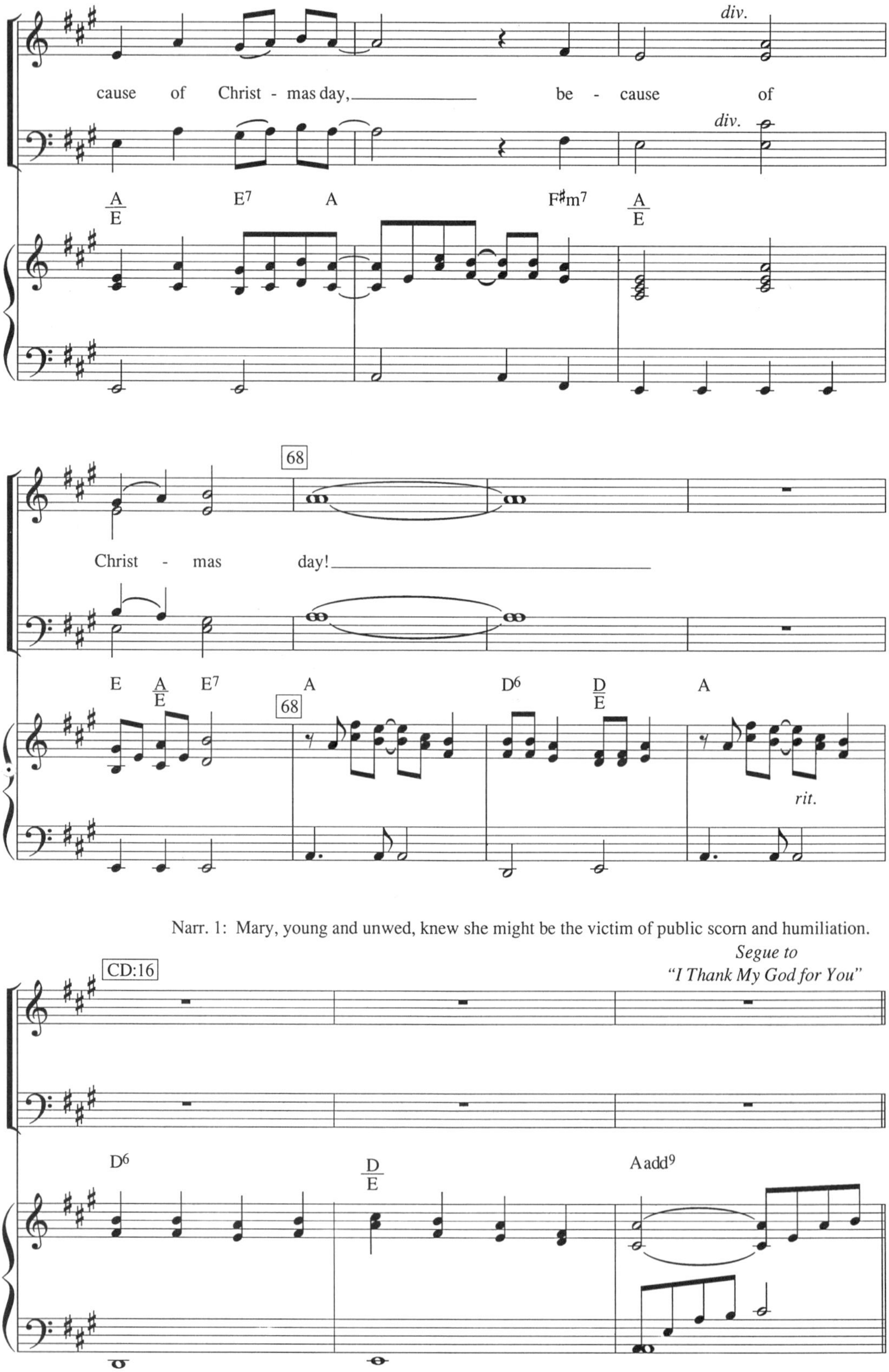

div.

cause of Christ - mas day, ______ be - cause of

div.

A/E E7 A F♯m7 A/E

68

Christ - mas day! ______

E A/E E7 A D6 D/E A

68

rit.

Narr. 1: Mary, young and unwed, knew she might be the victim of public scorn and humiliation.

Segue to "I Thank My God for You"

I Thank My God for You

Robin Wolaver

Bill Wolaver
Arr. by Bill Wolaver

Yet, without fear, she surrendered to the Lord's will and expressed these words of praise.

Narr. 2: "My soul glorifies the Lord and my spirit rejoices in God, my Savior." Narr. 1: Her obedience was richly

rewarded. One quiet night, in a small stable, God blessed her with the honor of giving birth to His Son.

* *For visual effect, a manger scene with Mary cradling the baby in her arms, may be used throughout this song.*

13
slight rit.
true, Chos-en by the Lord to bring to earth His pre-cious Son–
Gsus G G7/B Cm B♭/D E♭ A♭m6
slight rit.
more rit. 17 a tempo
cher-ished Rose of Shar-on, an-noint-ed One. And now she gent-ly rocks her
Prince of Peace, an-noint-ed One.
E♭sus/B♭ E♭/B♭ B♭/C Cm7 Fm9 Fm A♭/B♭ E♭add9
more rit.
a tempo
div.
Sav - ior, and looks with love in-to His ho-ly eyes. Her
div.
A♭m6/E♭ E♭add9 Gsus G G7/B

21
unis.
heart is filled with hap - pi - ness; her face is bright with joy. She whis - pers, oh so soft - ly, to her
Cm
B♭/D
E♭
A♭m6
E♭sus/B♭
E♭/B♭
B♭/C
Cm7
21
CD:18
slight rit.
mf
div.
27
a tempo
= ca. 76
pre - cious ba - by boy. I thank my God for
div.
Fm9
Fm
A♭/B♭
B♭7
E♭/B♭
Fm7
27
slight rit.
mf
a tempo
You, sweet lit - tle Child so new. God has been
B♭
E♭
B♭/D
Cm

31
good to me; He is rich in mer - cy.
31
Fm7 B♭ B♭sus/C B♭/D E♭add11/9 E♭
35
A song of joy I'll sing to praise my
E♭7 D♭/E♭ E♭7 A♭ E♭/G Fm B♭7
35
39 rit.
Lord and King. Al - le - lu - ia, al - le - lu,
E♭ D♭6 C7 C/E Fmadd11/9 Fm
39
rit.

CD:19
a tempo ♩ = 72
unis.
I thank my God for You.
unis.
B♭
A♭m6/E♭
E♭
a tempo
Solo (opt. choir unison)
44
mf
Mem-o-ries of how the an-gel told her are
B♭/C
C
F
B♭m6/F
44
mf
gath-ered like a trea-sure in her heart. And though she can-not see what to-
48
Fadd9
Asus
A
A7/C♯
Dm
C/E
48

slight rit.
50
CD:20
mor-row holds in store, she'll cher-ish ev-'ry mo-ment as a bless-ing from the Lord.
F
B♭m6
Fsus/C
F/C
C/D
Dm7
Gm9
Gm
slight rit.
Choir mf
div.
54
a tempo ♩ = 78
I thank my God for You, sweet lit-tle
div.
B♭/C
Gm7
C
mf a tempo
Child so new. God has been good to
58
F
C/E
Dm
Gm7

me; He is rich in mer - cy. A song of
C
Csus/D
C/E
F add11/9
F
F7
E♭/F
F7
62
joy I'll sing to praise my Lord and
B♭
F/A
Gm
C7
F
E♭6
King. Al - le - lu - ia, al - le - lu, I thank my
66
D7
D/F♯
Gm9
Gm
C

rit.
unis.
God for You.
I thank my
C♯°7
Dm
C6
B♭M9
Fadd9
A
rit.
73
a tempo ♩ = 72
God
I thank my God
for You.
mp
Gm7
B♭
C
C
F
73
a tempo
rit.
B♭m6
F
F
B♭m
F
F
rit.

Narr. 2: "Unto us a child is born, unto us a son is given, and the government will be on His shoulders.

Narr. 1: And He will be called 'Wonderful Counselor, Mighty God, Everlasting Father, Prince of Peace'."

Narr. 2: The prophet Isaiah spoke these words long before the birth of Christ, and for centuries *(music begins)* God's people waited for the prophecy to be fulfilled.

Narr. 1: Then one night, God sent a great host of angels to greet a few common shepherds with the good news of great joy:

"Today, in the town of David,
a Savior has been born to you;
He is Christ the Lord."

The world would have to wait no more; the Messiah and King had come!

Good News of Great Joy

with "Good News, Angels Are a-Singin'" and "Go, Tell It on the Mountain"

Robin Wolaver and Julie Adams

Bill Wolaver
Arr. by Bill Wolaver

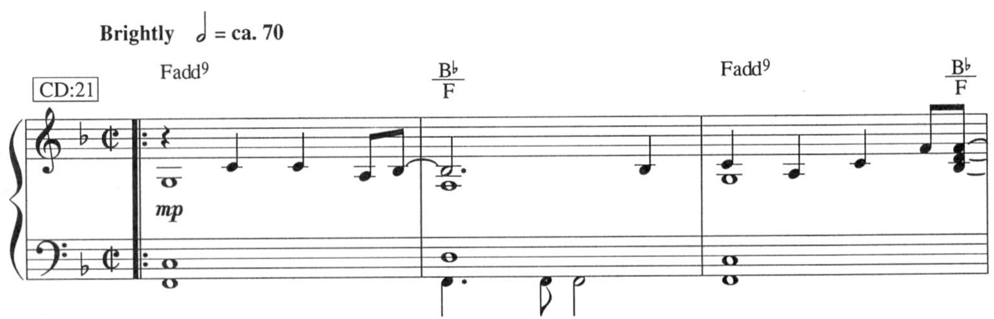

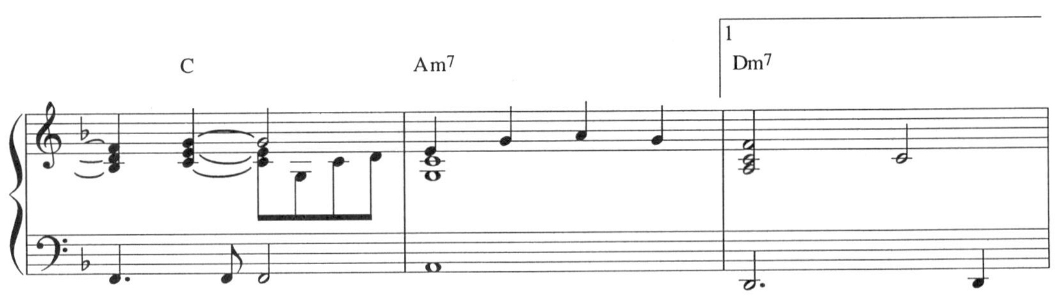

CD:22
12
Ladies unison
mp
Year af - ter year,
Gm7
B♭/C
Fadd9
mp
a prayer went up to heav - en–
B♭
Fadd9
B♭/F
C/F
18
"Show us the Prom - ised One".
18
Am7
Dm7
Gm7

20
mp
Tear af - ter tear was
Men unison
B♭/C
Fadd9
B♭/F
cried out to the Fa - ther,–
24
"When will Mes -
Fadd9
B♭/F
C/F
Am7
si - ah come?"
Dm7
Gm7
B♭/C
A/C♯

28
smoothly
Then one dark and qui - et night, a star lit up the sky.
28
Dm C B♭ F/A Gm7 B♭/C
smoothly
32
CD:23
The voice of hope and love was heard with -
C/F F F/E
32
Dm C B♭ F/A
div. mf
36
in an in - fant's cry. Good news! Good news
div.
Gm7 Am7 B♭ Dm/B Gm/C
36
F Gm/F F
(♭)
mf

unis.
div.
of great joy! The mar-vel-ous sto - ry un - folds. Good
Gm/F F Bb/D C/E F Gm/C
40
unis.
news! Good news of great joy, new life for the young and the old.
F Gm/F F Gm/F F Bb/D C/E D/F#
44
An - gels sing and men re - joice;
Gm7 F/A Gm/Bb Dm/B Csus C

48
div.
heav - en sent a ba - by boy. Good news! Good news! Good
div.
Gm7 F/A Gm/B♭ Dm/B Gm/C F Gm/F F Gm/F
48
CD:24
unis.
news of great joy!
unis.
C7sus Gm/C F B♭/F
52
div.
Prayer af - ter prayer was an - swered in a mo -
52 Gadd9 C/G Gadd9 C/G

56
unis.
- ment;
Je - sus, the Christ was
D/G
Bm7
Em7
here.
60
Care af - ter care
Am7
C/D
Gadd9
C6/G
was lift - ed up for - ev - er;
div.
Gadd9
C/G
D/G

64
Heav - en had seen each tear.
64
Bm7
Em7
Am7
68
smoothly
Now the joy - ful song was sung, the
div.
C/D
B/D♯
Em
Bm/D
C
G/B
68
smoothly
72
years of wait - ing past. Em - man - u - el, the
Am7
D
GM9
G
D/F♯
72
Em
D

CD:25
hope of earth, was born to us at last. Good
C G/B Am7 Bm7 C Em/C♯ Am/D
f
76
news! Good news of great joy! The mar-vel-ous sto - ry un -
unis.
G Am/G G Am/G G C/E D/F♯
folds. Good news! Good news of great joy, new
div.
81
G Am/D G Am/G G Am/G G
unis.

84
life for the young and the old.
An - gels sing and
C/E D/F♯ E/G♯ Am7 G/B Am/C
84
men re - joice;
heav - en sent a
ba - by boy. Good
div.
div.
Em/C♯ Dsus D Am7 G/B Am/C Em/C♯ Am/D
88 CD:26
unis.
news! Good news! Good news of great joy! Good
unis.
mf
88
G Am/G G Am/G D7sus Am/D G G/F

*"Good News, Angels Are a-Singin'" (Traditional Spiritual, new lyrics by Robin Wolaver)
91
div.
Good news, an-gels are a-sing-in'. Good news,
news, good news,
E♭ Fm/E♭ E♭ Fm/E♭ E♭ Fm/E♭ E♭ B♭ Cm/B♭ B♭7
an-gels are a-sing-in'. Good news,
95
unis.
an-gels are a-sing-in' that
Good news,
E♭ Fm/E♭ E♭ Fm/E♭ E♭ Fm/E♭ E♭ D°7 Cm A♭m6/C♭
**"Go, Tell It on the Mountain" (Traditional Spiritual)
99
Good news,
Je - sus Christ is born!
Go, tell it on the
E♭/B♭ Fm/B♭ E♭ A♭/B♭ E♭ Fm/E♭ E♭ Fm/E♭

div.
shep-herds are a-shout-in'. Good news, shep-herds are a-shout-in'. Good
moun - tain, o-ver the hills and ev - 'ry - where.
E♭ Fm/E♭ E♭ B♭ Cm/B♭ B♭7 E♭ Fm/E♭ E♭
103
CD:27
news, shep-herds are a-shout-in' that Je - sus Christ is born.
Go, tell it on the moun - tain that Je - sus Christ is born.
div.
103
E♭ Fm/E♭ E♭ Fm/E♭ E♭ D°7 Cm A♭m6/C♭ E♭/B♭ Fm/B♭ E♭
107
f
Good news, heav-en is re-joic-in'.
Good news, good
unis. f
B♭/C
107
F Gm/F F Gm/F F Gm/F F
f

111
Good news, heav-en is re-joic-in'. Good news,
news, Good news,
C Dm/C C7 F Gm/F F 111 Gm/F F Gm/F
mf
unis. div.
115
heav-en is re-joic-in' that Je-sus Christ is born! Good news,
heav-en is re-joic-in' that Je-sus Christ is born! Go, tell it on the
div. unis.
F E°7 Dm B♭m6/D♭ F/C Gm/C F C/D 115 G
118
glo-ry, hal-le-lu-jah. Good news, glo-ry, hal-le-lu-jah. Good
moun-tain, o-ver the hills and ev-'ry-where.
opt. div.
G D7 118 G Am/G

CD:28
news,
glo - ry, hal - le - lu - jah that
Je - sus Christ is born!
Go, tell it on the moun - tain that
Je - sus Christ is born!
div.
G
Em
Cm6
E♭
G
D
Am
D
G
ff
124
Good news! Good news
124
C
D
Am
D
G
Am
G
G
ff
unis.
of great joy!
The mar-vel-ous sto - ry un - folds.
Good
div.
unis.
div.
Am
G
G
C
E
D
F♯
G
Am
D

128
unis.
news! Good news of great joy, new life for the young and the old.
unis.
G Am/G G Am/G G C/E D/F♯ E/G♯
132
An - gels sing and men re - joice;
Am7 G/B Am/C Em/C♯ Dsus D
heav - en sent a ba - by boy. Good news! Good news! Good
136
Am7 G/B Am/C Em/C♯ Am/D G Am/G G Am/G

div.
news! Good news! Good news! Good news! Good
div.
D7sus
Am
D
G
Am
G
G
Am
G
D7sus
Am
D
140
news! Good news! Good news
of great joy,
140
G
Am
G
G
Am
G
D7sus
Am
D
G
fff
of great joy,
of great joy!
Am
D
G
Am7
D
G
fff

What Did the Angels Say?

with "Angels, from the Realms of Glory" and "Angels We Have Heard on High"

Nancy Gordon and Robin Wolaver

Bill Wolaver
Arr. by Bill Wolaver

Slowly, with freedom ♩ = ca. 76

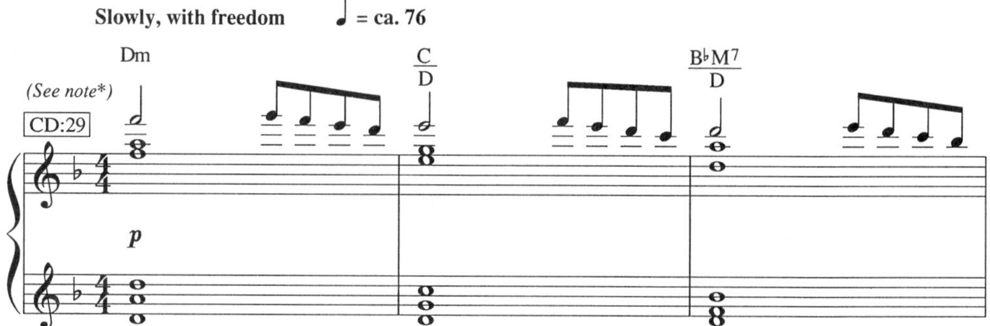

Narr. 1: The shepherds could not contain the joy that filled their hearts when they saw the Savior. They went about

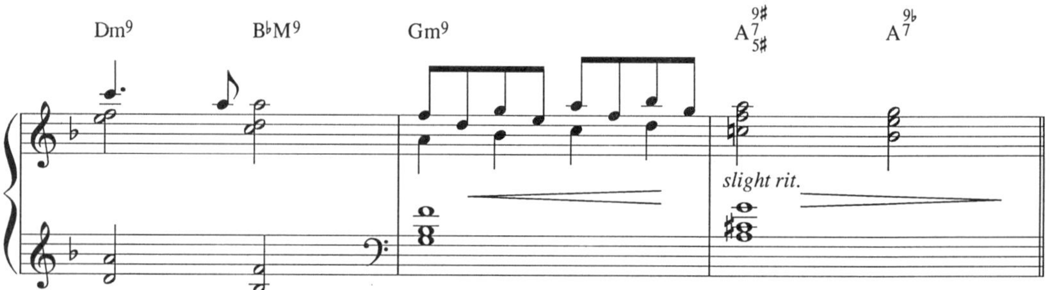

telling everyone what the angel had said to them about the Child, and all who heard it were amazed.

Dramatically, march-like ♩ = 88

* *For dramatic effect, costuming may be used. Also, two or three 'shepherds' may accompany the soloist in a supporting role.*

ran to Beth - le - hem, and there with - in a cat - tle stall the ho - ly Child we found. Our
div. f
Beth - le - hem.
Ah
div.
C G D/F♯ Em D D/F♯ D G G/B G

43
hearts were filled with won - der when we saw the ho - ly One. Now
Ah
Now
43
C D Bm Em

we must spread the good news: "Em - man - u - el has
we must spread the good news: "Em - man - u - el has
D
C
B
Em
B
B7
CD:34
47
come!"
come!"
47
Esus
E
D
Csus
C

* "Angels, from the Realms of Glory" (James Montgomery-Henry T. Smart)
49
ff
Come and wor - ship, come and wor - ship,
F
B♭/D B♭sus/C B♭ D7/A Gm Dm/F E♭ B♭/D
rit.
Brightly ♩ = 116
CD:35
wor - ship Christ, the new - born King!
Cm B♭/D Cm/E♭ C7/E B♭/F F
B♭ F B♭ F/A Gm7 F/A

B♭
F
B♭
F/A
Gm
F
Csus
B♭/C
* "Angels We Have Heard on High" (French Carol)
56
mf
An - gels we have heard on high,
56
tacet
F
C
F
B♭/C
F
mf
f
59
Sweet - ly sing - ing o'er the plains;
59
tacet
Dm
A
Dm
A
Dm
mf
f

62
And the moun - tains in re - ply,
62
tacet
mf
F C F Bb/C F
f
67
f
Ech - o - ing their joy - ous strains. Come to Beth - le -
tacet
F C7/E C/D D
67
G G/B
f
hem and see Him whose birth the an - gels sing;
Gsus/A G D G D G G/B G D/F# Em D

71
CD:36
Come a - dore on bend - ed knee Christ the Lord, the
71
G G/B Gsus/A G D G D G G/B
75
ff
new - born King. Glo - - -
G/D D C/G G
75
G G/F E E/G♯ Am Am/G D/F♯ D
ff
1
- - ri - a in ex - cel - sis
G G/F♯ C/E C D Dsus/E D/F♯ E D C
1
G/B D G C/E

2

De - o! in ex - cel - sis De - o,

f

G/D Em7 D/F♯ D

2 G/B tacet

f

83

f

in ex - cel - sis De - o, in ex - cel - sis

ff

83

D D/C G/B D G C/E

ff

87

De - o!

G/D D

87 G tacet

R.H.

G N.C.

Narr. 1: Let's pause a moment and quietly reflect on the beauty of the Christ Child and the significance of His birth. That tiny babe, so fragile and delicate, was God Himself. He came to live among us that we might know Him and understand how deeply He loves us.

Narr. 2: It is the power of His love that moves us to look beyond ourselves, and to take the good news of Christmas to all people. *(music begins)* Rich or poor, captive or free, young or old, the deepest need of every heart is to hear the words "God loves you, and has given His Son to be your Savior."

Narr. 1: This is the heart of Christmas, the "good news of great joy" that reaches around the world, changing lives that are broken and empty into lives of wholeness and peace. The Christmas story is only the beginning of our message... but what a magnificent place to start!

Christmas, for Every Heart

with "All Over the World," "Joy to the World," and Reprise-"Good News of Great Joy"

Robin Wolaver

Bill Wolaver
Arr. by Bill Wolaver

CD:38
Gadd9
Cm6/G
Ladies unison (opt. duet)
Some -
13
Gadd9
mp
D/G
Cadd9/G
Cm6/G
where a - cross the o - cean wide a fam - 'ly trims the tree, and
Bm7
div.
Em7
Am7
D7sus
D
unis.
lights a spe - cial can - dle for ev - 'ry - one to see; And
17
Gadd9
Dadd9/F♯
Cadd9/E
div.
D♯°7
in a land where Sa - tan's hand has si - lenced free - dom's voice, be -

CD:39
unis.
liev - ers soft - ly cel - e-brate and in their hearts re - joice. A
Add men unison mp
Em D Cadd9 11# C G/B Am7 C/D D
21
lit - tle face with skin of bronze is glow - ing with His light, and
chil - dren of God's fam - i - ly we stand in one ac - cord, to
Gadd9 D/G Cadd9/G Cm6/G
alto opt.
eyes of blue so ea - ger - ly a - wait that spe - cial night. For
cel - e-brate His glo - rious grace, one hope, one faith, one Lord. And
Bm7 Em7 Am7 D7sus D

25

ev - 'ry man - made bar - ri - er___ was bro - ken by His birth. His
e - ven though tra - di - tions change___ in lands that are be - yond,

div.

Gadd9 Dadd9/F♯ D/F♯ Cadd9/E C/E D♯°7

CD:40
CD:42 *(2nd time)*

love tran - scends our dif - f'renc - es and of - fers peace on
Je - sus is our com - mon ground, His love our com - mon

Em D Cadd9 11♯ C G/B Am7

rit. **mf** 30 *slightly faster* ♩ = ca. 63

earth. It's mer - ry Christ - mas, O come all ye
bond.

D7sus D7 Gadd9 Bm7 G/B

slightly faster

rit. **mf**

faith - ful. Mer - ry Christ - mas, sing joy to the
G/C C Am7 D13 Gadd9 Dm7 F/G G7
world. Hearts u - nite to spread the light of
34
CM7 Gadd9/B Am7 Dsus D/C
unis.
love both near and far. It's mer - ry
rit. (1st time only)
Gadd9/B G/B Cm/E♭

1
♩ = 60
CD:41
Christ - mas for ev - 'ry heart.
G/D
Am/D
D13
Gadd9
3
2
CD:43
2. As Christ - mas for ev - 'ry
Cm6/G
G/D
Am7/D
CM7/D
f
42
heart. It's mer - ry Christ-mas, O come all ye
Bm7/E
A
C♯m7
A/C♯

div.
faith - ful. Mer - ry Christ - mas, sing joy to the
div.
A/D D Bm7 E13 Aadd9 Em7 G/A A7
46
world. Hearts u - nite to spread the light of
DM7 Aadd9/C♯ Bm7 Esus E/D
46
3
rit.
love both near and far. It's mer - ry
Aadd9/C♯ A/C♯ Dm/F
3
rit.

49
slightly slower
It's mer - ry
Christ - mas for ev - 'ry heart.
A/E Bm7/E C♯/E♯ F♯madd9 F♯m Dm6/F
Christ - mas for ev - 'ry
Mer - ry Christ - mas for ev - 'ry
A/E E/F♯ F♯m7 Bm7 E13
53 CD:44 slight accel.
unis.
Slightly faster 𝅗𝅥 = 63
heart.
A A/G F Gm7
slight accel.
mf

*"All Over the World" (Phill McHugh-Greg Nelson)
With strength
57
All o - ver the world, all o - ver the world,
All o - ver the world,
F/A F
57 B♭
With strength
Asus A/C♯
61
all o - ver the world,
God's Spir - it is mov - ing
Dm Dm/C B♭
61 C/B♭
all o - ver the world. All o - ver the world,
all o - ver the world.
F/A Gm C C/B♭ F/A

65
all o - ver the world,
All o - ver the world,
all o - ver the world,
65
B♭
Asus
A/C♯
Dm
Dm/C
div.
unis.
God's Spir - it is mov - ing with pow'r
all o - ver the world.
div.
unis.
B♭
F/A
B♭
B♭/C
71
div.
God's Spir - it is mov - ing with pow'r
div.
71
Dm
Dm/C
B♭
F/C

76
*"Joy to the World!" (Watts-Handel)
CD:45
molto rit.
all o - ver the world!
ff Faster 𝅗𝅥 = 72
all o - ver the, Joy to the
all o - ver the world.
ff
all o - ver the, Joy to the
B♭/C
76
D
A/D
G/D
molto rit.
ff Faster
8va
world! the Lord is come. Let earth re -
80
world!
D
D/F♯
G
D/A
A7
Dsus/E D/F♯ Dsus/E D
G
80
8va
8va
unis.
ceive her King. Let
A/G
D/F♯
Em7
D
D/C
B
A
8va

84
mf
ev - 'ry heart pre - pare Him room, And
unis.
84
Dsus/G
Dadd9/F♯
Dsus/E
Dsus/A
D
Bm
8va
loco
88
building
heav'n and na - ture sing, And heav'n and na - ture
88
D/A
A
mf building (accented and pulsating)
f
92
div.
sing, And heav'n, and heav'n and
div.
A/G
92
D/F♯
G
D/A
A♯°7 Bm Bm/A G
f

unis.
na - ture sing. And
unis.
D/A F♯7/A♯ Bm Gm add9/B♭ Gm/B♭
97
heav'n, and heav -
div.
div.
97
D/A D/C G/B F♯/A♯ F♯ F♯/A♯ F♯7/C♯
slight rit.
en and na - ture
Bm G D/A Asus A
slight rit.

103
Driving (♩=138)
CD:46
sing!
Dsus
D
Dsus/C
D/C
Gadd9/B
G/B
F♯m/C♯
A7/C♯
Driving
*"Good News of Great Joy" (Bill and Robin Wolaver-Julie Adams)
f
107
unis.
Good news! Good news of great joy! The
Cadd9/D
Am/D
G
Am/G
marvel-ous sto-ry un-folds. Good news! Good news
div.
111
C/E
D/F♯

unis.
of great joy, new life for the young and the old.
unis.
Am/G G C/E D/F♯ E/G♯
115
An - gels sing and men re - joice; heav - en sent a ba - by boy. Good
115
Am7 G/B Am/C Em/C♯ Dsus D Am7 G/B Am/C Em/C♯ Am/D
119
div.
news! Good news! Good news! Good news! Good news! Good news! Good
div.
119
G Am/G G Am/G D7sus Am/D G Am/G G Am/G D7sus Am/D

news! Good news! Good news of great joy,
G Am/G G D7sus Am/D G
126
of great joy, of great joy!
126
Am/D G C/D Am/D G Am/G G Am/G G
Am/G G Am/G G Am/G G Am/G G